Low fat

A Pyramid Cookery Paperback

Low fat

hamlyn

An Hachette Livre UK Company
www.hachettelivre.co.uk

A Pyramid Paperback

First published in Great Britain in 2007 by
Hamlyn, a division of Octopus Publishing Group Ltd
2-4 Heron Quays, London E14 4JP

This edition published 2008

The material in this book has appeared in the following
books published by Hamlyn: *Cooking for a Healthy Heart*
(Jacqui Lynas, 1998), *Delicious Food for Diabetics*
(Louise Blair, 2005), *Gourmet Low Carb* (Sara Lewis, 2005),
Kitchen Library Low Fat (Sally Mansfield, 1998), *Low Fat*
(1999), *Low Fat High Flavour* (1997), *Low GI Food for
Friends* (Azmina Govindji, 2006).

ISBN 978-0-600-61887-4

A CIP catalogue record for this book is available from
the British Library

Printed and bound in China

10 9 8 7 6 5 4 3 2 1

Notes

Both metric and imperial measurements have been
given in all recipes. Use one set of measurements only
and not a mixture of both.

Meat and poultry should be cooked thoroughly.
To test if poultry is cooked, pierce the flesh through
the thickest part with a skewer or fork – the juices
should run clear, never pink or red.

This book includes dishes made with nuts and nut
derivatives. It is advisable for those with known
allergic reactions to nuts and nut derivatives and
those who may be potentially vulnerable to these
allergies, such as pregnant and nursing mothers,
invalids, the elderly, babies and children, to avoid
dishes made with nuts and nut oils. It is also prudent
to check the labels of pre-prepared ingredients for
the possible inclusion of nut derivatives.

The Department of Health advises that eggs should
not be consumed raw. This book contains some
dishes made with raw or lightly cooked eggs.
It is prudent for more vulnerable people, such as
pregnant and nursing mothers, invalids, the elderly,
babies and young children, to avoid uncooked or
lightly cooked dishes made with eggs.

All the recipes in this book have been analysed by
a professional nutritionist. The analysis refers to a
single serving.

Contents

Introduction

Low fat, high flavour

Many people assume that low-fat food won't taste good. They think that they will have to compromise on flavour and won't be able to enjoy a meal as much as they used to. Of course, this is complete nonsense – in fact, the opposite is often true. Because some ingredients are limited or absent in low-fat recipes, the dishes tend to be more creative and include other wonderful flavourings as substitutes for butter, cream and oils. Low-fat recipes contain plenty of aromatic spices, fragrant fresh herbs and citrus flavourings; and the abundance of seasonal fruit and vegetables, beans and pulses, fish and lean meat should mean that you end up with a wide repertoire of flavour-packed recipes at your fingertips.

This book brings together a selection of delicious dishes that should appeal to everyone. You really won't know that you are eating a low-fat meal, and, because so many of them are quick and simple to prepare, they are easy to fit in with a busy lifestyle. You won't have to spend hours preparing food, yet you will be able to eat delicious, healthy meals every day.

Low-fat living

A low-fat diet should be about much more than a few changes in your eating habits. If you are really going to appreciate the benefits that a new food regime will bring, you need to combine it with positive alterations to your whole lifestyle. Whether the idea is to lose a little excess weight, to have more energy or to feel generally healthier, you should ideally combine a well-balanced diet with regular exercise. It is not enough simply to eat properly: you also need to get your heart rate going, to kick-start your metabolism and to enhance your overall wellbeing.

The decision to switch to a low-fat diet should, therefore, be part of a broader attempt to improve your lifestyle. Even if you start with something easy – taking up an exercise class or getting off the bus one stop earlier and walking the rest of the way, for example – you'll feel much better for it. Once you have made a few simple changes to your diet and lifestyle you will soon reap the benefits and be getting into good habits that will last a lifetime.

Cooking culture

There are a number of simple rules to remember when you switch to a low-fat diet, and, whether you are following a recipe, eating out in a restaurant or just rustling up a sandwich, it's good to have these stored away somewhere in your memory. Of course, all good rules are made to be broken once in a while, and life would be extremely dull without the odd treat or two. So don't deprive yourself of the occasional piece of cake or square of chocolate. As long as these really are just treats, you can look forward to them.

Try to keep the following guidelines in mind when you are choosing recipes to cook and deciding on the foods to buy for your storecupboard.

Cut down on saturated fat

We all need a certain amount of fat in our diet, but it's important to eat the right kind. Saturated fat can result in an increased cholesterol level, and this is something to avoid as far as possible. Banish high-fat foods and snacks and try to avoid cooking with butter or lard. Unsaturated fats are usually vegetable based, and these are the better option for cooking. Take a tip from the Mediterranean cuisine and use olive oil for cooking.

Switch to low-fat versions

Here's an easy way to cut down on fat right away. Simply buy lower fat versions of your usual milk and yogurt, and buy cottage cheese instead of Cheddar for your sandwiches and baked potatoes. Low fat crème fraîche and yogurt are great alternatives to cream.

Eat healthy snacks

Snacking between meals doesn't have to be a bad thing. A piece of fruit or wholemeal toast will give you a much-needed energy boost in the middle of the afternoon. If you work in an office, try keeping a bowl of dried fruit and nuts on your desk so that you don't give in to the temptation of snacking on crisps or biscuits.

Ban the frying pan

Grill or oven-bake fish and chicken and steam vegetables to lock in all the goodness. You can buy electric steamers that have a number of food compartments or, alternatively, use a stacking steamer that will fit over a saucepan and give equally good results.

Plan your meals

We're often told not to go shopping on an empty stomach, because there will be more temptation to fill the trolley with treats. By the same token, it's advisable not to go shopping without some idea of the meals you'll be preparing. You can't plan for every last recipe and snack, of course, but it's worth taking a few minutes to think about some main meals and list the ingredients. That way you know you'll have everything you need before you start cooking.

The recipes that follow show the great range of flavours and ingredients that can be enjoyed while you are maintaining a low-fat diet. There are ideas for starters, fish and seafood, meat and vegetarian options, as well as a number of desserts. Treat yourself to mouth-watering dishes such as Lemon Grass Fish Skewers (see page 54), Venison Casserole (see page 84) and Rocket Risotto (see page 98), and enjoy fantastic-tasting food as you work towards a new, healthier lifestyle.

Side dishes
and starters

Red pepper and ginger soup

Preparation time **20 minutes**,
  plus cooling
Cooking time **45 minutes**
Serves **4**

3 red peppers, halved, cored and
  deseeded
1 red onion, quartered
2 garlic cloves, unpeeled
1 teaspoon olive oil
5 cm (2 inches) fresh root ginger,
  peeled and grated
1 teaspoon ground cumin
1 teaspoon ground coriander
1 large potato, chopped
900 ml (1½ pints) vegetable stock
salt and pepper
4 tablespoons low-fat fromage
  frais, to serve

1 Place the peppers, onion and garlic in a nonstick roasting tin. Roast in a preheated oven, 200°C (400°F), Gas Mark 6, for 40 minutes or until the peppers have blistered and the onion and garlic are soft. If the onion quarters start to brown too much, cover them with the pepper halves.

2 Meanwhile, heat the oil in a saucepan and fry the ginger, cumin and coriander over a low heat for 1–2 minutes or until softened. Add the potato and stir well, season to taste with salt and pepper and pour in the stock. Cover and simmer for 30 minutes.

3 Remove the vegetables from the oven. Place the peppers in a polythene bag, tie the top and leave to cool. (The steam produced in the bag makes it easier to remove the skin when the peppers are cool.) Add the onions to the potato mixture and carefully squeeze out the garlic pulp into the saucepan. Peel the peppers and add all but one half to the soup. Simmer for 5 minutes.

4 Pour the soup into a liquidizer or food processor, and blend, in batches if necessary, for a few seconds until the mixture is quite smooth. Alternatively, rub the soup through a sieve to purée. Return to the saucepan and, if necessary, thin with a little water to achieve the desired consistency.

5 Spoon the soup into warm bowls. Slice the remaining pepper half and arrange a little on top of each bowl of soup with a spoonful of fromage frais.

Fat 2 g
Carbohydrate 21 g
Protein 6 g
Energy 112 kcal (473 kj)

Butternut squash and rosemary soup

Preparation time **15 minutes**
Cooking time **1 hour 10 minutes**
Serves **4**

1 butternut squash
a few sprigs of rosemary, plus
    extra to garnish
150 g (5 oz) red lentils, washed
1 onion, finely chopped
900 ml (1½ pints) vegetable stock
salt and pepper

1 Halve the squash and use a spoon to scoop out the seeds and fibrous flesh. Cut the squash into small chunks and put the pieces in a nonstick roasting tin. Sprinkle over the rosemary and season to taste with salt and pepper. Roast in a preheated oven, 200°C (400°F), Gas Mark 6, for 45 minutes.

2 Meanwhile, place the lentils in a saucepan. Cover with water, then bring to the boil and boil rapidly for 10 minutes. Strain, return the lentils to a clean saucepan with the onion and stock and simmer for 5 minutes. Season to taste.

3 Remove the squash from the oven and scoop the flesh from the skin. Mash the flesh with a fork and add it to the soup. Simmer the soup for 25 minutes then ladle it into warm bowls. Garnish with more rosemary before serving.

Fat 1 g
Carbohydrate 26 g
Protein 10 g
Energy 146 kcal (614 kj)

Quick and easy miso soup

Preparation time **5 minutes**
Cooking time **10 minutes**
Serves **4**

900 ml (1½ pints) vegetable stock
2 tablespoons miso paste
125 g (4 oz) shiitake mushrooms,
    sliced
200 g (7 oz) tofu (beancurd),
    cubed

1 Place the stock in a saucepan and heat until it is simmering.

2 Add the miso paste, shiitake mushrooms and tofu (beancurd) to the stock and simmer for 5 minutes. Ladle the soup into warm bowls and serve.

Fat 3 g
Carbohydrate 2 g
Protein 6 g
Energy 56 kcal (231 kj)

Hot and sour mushroom soup

Preparation time **5 minutes**
Cooking time **15 minutes**
Serves **4**

1.2 litres (2 pints) fish stock
1 lemon grass stalk, lightly crushed
3 fresh kaffir lime leaves or
   3 pieces of lime rind
2 Thai red chillies, halved
   and deseeded
2 tablespoons lime juice
2 tablespoons Thai fish sauce
50 g (2 oz) can bamboo shoots
125 g (4 oz) oyster mushrooms
2 spring onions, finely sliced
½ red chilli, sliced, to garnish

1 Pour the stock into a saucepan and add the lemon grass, lime leaves or rind, and chillies. Simmer for 10 minutes.

2 Strain the liquid into a clean saucepan. Reserve a little red chilli and discard the remaining seasonings. Add the lime juice and fish sauce to the soup with the bamboo shoots and mushrooms and reserved chilli.

3 Simmer the soup for 5 minutes, then spoon it into warm bowls and sprinkle with the spring onions. Serve garnished with red chilli slices.

Fat 0 g
Carbohydrate 3 g
Protein 2 g
Energy 23 kcal (97 kj)

Roast root vegetable soup

Preparation time **10 minutes**
Cooking time **1 hour 5 minutes**
Serves **6**

4 carrots, chopped
2 parsnips, chopped
1 leek, finely chopped
1.2 litres (2 pints) vegetable stock
2 teaspoons thyme leaves
salt and pepper
sprigs of thyme, to garnish

1 Place the carrots and parsnips in a nonstick roasting tin, season to taste with salt and pepper and roast in a preheated oven, 200°C (400°F), Gas Mark 6, for 1 hour or until the vegetables are soft.

2 About 20 minutes before the vegetables have finished roasting, put the leek in a large saucepan with the stock and 1 teaspoon thyme. Simmer, covered, for 20 minutes.

3 Transfer the roasted root vegetables to a liquidizer or food processor and blend (or rub through a sieve), adding a little of the stock if necessary. Transfer the vegetable purée to the saucepan and check the seasoning. Add the remaining thyme, stir the soup and simmer for 5 minutes.

4 Ladle the soup into warm bowls and serve garnished with thyme sprigs.

Fat 1 g
Carbohydrate 12 g
Protein 2 g
Energy 60 kcal (254 kj)

Baked field mushrooms

Preparation time **5 minutes**
Cooking time **40 minutes**
Serves **4**

5 large field or open cap
   mushrooms
4 tablespoons balsamic vinegar
1 tablespoon wholegrain mustard
75 g (3 oz) watercress
salt and pepper
shavings of Parmesan cheese,
   to garnish (optional)

1 Remove and reserve the stalks from 4 of the mushrooms. Place the 4 mushrooms, skin side down, in a small nonstick roasting tin and cook in a preheated oven, 200°C (400°F), Gas Mark 6, for 15 minutes.

2 Meanwhile, make the dressing. Finely chop the remaining mushroom and the reserved stalks and mix them in a small bowl with the vinegar and mustard. Season to taste with salt and pepper.

3 Remove the mushrooms from the oven and spoon some dressing over each one. Return the mushrooms to the oven and continue to cook for 25 minutes, covering the tin with foil after 10 minutes.

4 When the mushrooms are cooked, transfer them to a plate and keep warm. Tip the watercress into the hot juices and toss well. Spoon piles of watercress on to 4 warmed plates. Place a mushroom on top and garnish with Parmesan shavings, if using.

Fat 3 g
Carbohydrate 1 g
Protein 4 g
Energy 42 kcal (177 kj)

Mediterranean peppers

Preparation time **10 minutes**
Cooking time **1 hour**
Serves **4**

2 red and 2 yellow peppers, halved,
   cored and deseeded but stems
   left intact
24 cherry tomatoes, halved
2 garlic cloves, thinly sliced
40 g (1½ oz) capers in brine,
   drained and rinsed
1 bunch of basil
25 ml (1 fl oz) olive oil
pepper
mixed salad leaves, to serve

1 Put the mixed peppers, cut side up, in a shallow baking dish. Divide the halved cherry tomatoes, garlic slivers and capers among the pepper halves. Add a few basil leaves, then lightly drizzle each pepper with olive oil and season with pepper.

2 Pour about 300 ml (½ pint) water into the base of the dish to prevent the peppers from sticking. Cover the dish tightly with foil and cook in a preheated oven, 180°C (350°F), Gas Mark 4, for 20 minutes. Remove the foil, reduce the temperature to 150°C (300°F), Gas Mark 2, and bake for another 40 minutes or until the peppers are soft.

3 Garnish the peppers with the remaining basil leaves and serve with mixed salad leaves.

Fat 8 g
Carbohydrate 10 g
Protein 5 g
Energy 128 kcal (535 kj)

Griddled aubergines with chilli toasts

Preparation time **15 minutes**
Cooking time **10 minutes**
Serves **4**

2 aubergines, about 550 g
 (1 lb 2 oz) in total
2 teaspoons olive oil
50 g (2 oz) sun-blush tomatoes
2 garlic cloves, crushed
4 tablespoons lemon juice
pepper
basil leaves, to garnish

Chilli toasts
4 slices multigrain bread
1 tablespoon chilli-infused oil

1 Cut the aubergines lengthways into 5 mm (¼ inch) slices and season with black pepper.

2 Prepare the chilli toast. Remove the crusts from each slice of bread and cut the bread into two neat triangles. Brush each side of the bread with the chilli-infused oil, put the bread on a baking sheet and cook in a preheated oven, 220°C (425°F), Gas Mark 7, for 8–10 minutes until crisp and golden.

3 Meanwhile, oil a ridged griddle pan and heat it. Put the aubergine slices and tomatoes on the pan with the garlic and cook for about 4 minutes until they start to soften. Turn over the aubergines and cook for a further 4 minutes. Finally, sprinkle over the lemon juice.

4 Remove the chilli toasts from the oven and serve with the aubergine and tomato piled high in the centre of each plate. Garnish with the basil leaves and sprinkle with extra pepper.

Fat 6 g
Carbohydrate 15 g
Protein 4 g
Energy 122 kcal (513 kj)

Red lentil dhal with cucumber raita

Preparation time **15 minutes**
Cooking time **30 minutes**
Serves **4**

225 g (7½ oz) red lentils
1 tablespoon rapeseed oil
1 large onion, finely chopped
2 garlic cloves, crushed
1 teaspoon crushed fresh
    root ginger
2 green chillies, deseeded and
    finely chopped
4 tomatoes, finely chopped
½ teaspoon ground turmeric
1½ teaspoons garam masala
450 ml (¾ pint) hot water
4 tablespoons lemon juice
50 g (2 oz) coriander leaves and
    stems, chopped
salt
pitta breads, to serve

Raita
10 cm (4 inches) cucumber, grated
450 ml (¾ pint) reduced-fat
    natural yogurt
1 teaspoon cumin seeds
½ teaspoon black pepper

To garnish
3 spring onions, green stems only,
    sliced diagonally
½ teaspoon red chilli powder

1 Soak the lentils in a bowl of warm water. Heat the oil in a large, nonstick frying pan with a lid and stir-fry the onion, garlic, ginger and chillies for 3–5 minutes. Stir in the tomatoes and cook, stirring from time to time, until the tomatoes begin to go mushy. Add the turmeric and garam masala. Cover and simmer, stirring occasionally, for 5 minutes.

2 Drain the lentils and add them, with the measured hot water, to the frying pan. Stir well, cover and cook for 15–20 minutes until the lentils are tender but not mushy. Add a little more water if the mixture becomes too dry.

3 Meanwhile, make the raita. Drain the grated cucumber on kitchen paper and place this in a bowl with all the other ingredients and stir to mix. Chill until ready to serve.

4 When the dhal is cooked, stir in salt to taste, lemon juice and coriander. Garnish with the spring onions and sprinkle red chilli powder over the raita. Serve with pitta breads.

Fat 5 g
Carbohydrate 48 g
Protein 22 g
Energy 316 kcal (1336 kj)

Bloody Mary jellies with miniature salad garnish

Preparation time **20 minutes**, plus chilling
Cooking time **4–5 minutes**
Serves **6**

3 tablespoons water
3 teaspoons powdered gelatine
½ cucumber
½ red pepper, cored and deseeded
¼ red onion
1 celery stick, with leaves
1 tomato
400 ml (14 fl oz) tomato juice
3 tablespoons vodka
8 teaspoons Worcestershire sauce
Tabasco or chilli sauce, to taste
salt and pepper

1 Put the water in a small, heatproof bowl and sprinkle the gelatine over the top, making sure that all the dry powder is absorbed. Set aside for 5 minutes.

2 Cut off and reserve a slice, 2.5 cm (1 inch) thick, from the cucumber. Pare away half the rind from the remaining cucumber and discard. Roughly chop the cucumber flesh and purée it with the red pepper and two-thirds of the red onion in a liquidizer or food processor until smooth.

3 Finely dice the reserved cucumber slice, the remaining red onion, the celery stick and leaves and the tomato, and reserve for garnish.

4 Stand the bowl of gelatine in a small saucepan, half-filled with water, and simmer for 4–5 minutes until the gelatine has dissolved.

5 Mix the puréed vegetables with the tomato juice, vodka and 4 teaspoons of the Worcestershire sauce. Mix in Tabasco or chilli sauce and salt and pepper to taste. Gradually stir in the dissolved gelatine in a thin, steady trickle. Pour the tomato mixture into 6 small moulds and chill for 4 hours or until set.

6 Dip each mould in hot water, count to five and then loosen the top and invert the mould on to a serving plate. Holding the mould and plate, shake to release and lift off the mould. Spoon the finely diced vegetables around the jellies and serve drizzled with the remaining Worcestershire sauce.

Fat 0 g
Carbohydrate 5 g
Protein 2 g
Energy 44 kcal (187 kj)

Bulgar wheat salad with spiced yogurt

Preparation time **20 minutes**,
   plus soaking and resting
Serves **2**

125 g (4 oz) bulgar wheat
4 large plums, pitted and each cut
   into about 8 slices
1 garlic clove, crushed
1 red onion, finely chopped
25 g (1 oz) flat leaf parsley,
   chopped
handful of mint, chopped
2 tablespoons olive oil
4 tablespoons lemon juice
salt and pepper

Spiced yogurt
4 tablespoons low-fat
   natural yogurt
1 garlic clove, crushed
½ teaspoon cayenne pepper
½ teaspoon tomato purée
finely chopped chives, to garnish

1 Put the bulgar wheat in a large bowl, cover it with water and leave for 30 minutes to swell up. Drain any excess water from the bulgar wheat and squeeze it dry with your hands.

2 Mix all the other ingredients into the bulgar wheat, then put the salad in the refrigerator to rest for at least 30 minutes to allow the flavours to develop.

3 Make the spiced yogurt by mixing together all the ingredients. Serve the bulgar wheat salad accompanied by the spiced yogurt in individual bowls, garnished with finely chopped chives.

Fat 7 g
Carbohydrate 38 g
Protein 6 g
Energy 230 kcal (965 kj)

Chickpea and olive salad

Preparation time **10 minutes**
Serves **4**

250 g (8 oz) can chickpeas, drained
50 g (2 oz) pitted black olives,
    halved
½ red onion, finely chopped
150 g (5 oz) cherry tomatoes,
    halved
3 tablespoons chopped flat leaf
    parsley, plus extra to garnish
50 g (2 oz) watercress leaves,
    to serve

Yogurt dressing
1 garlic clove, crushed
100 ml (3½ fl oz) low-fat
    Greek yogurt
juice of ½ lime
pepper

1 First make the dressing. Mix together the garlic, yogurt and lime juice. Season to taste with pepper.

2 Stir together the chickpeas, olives, onion, tomatoes and parsley. Add the dressing to the chickpea mixture and mix thoroughly.

3 Serve the salad on a bed of watercress leaves, garnished with chopped parsley.

Fat 4 g
Carbohydrate 33 g
Protein 7 g
Energy 122 kcal (516 kj)

Lentil salad with green salsa

Preparation time **15 minutes**
Cooking time **45 minutes**
Serves **4**

1 teaspoon olive oil
1 small onion, finely chopped
300 g (10 oz) Puy lentils
450 ml (¾ pint) vegetable stock
200 g (7 oz) cherry tomatoes,
   chopped
1 bunch of spring onions, shredded
4 chapattis or flat breads, toasted,
   to serve

Green salsa
4 tablespoons chopped mixed
   herbs (such as parsley, coriander
   and chives)
1 tablespoon capers, drained
2 anchovy fillets (optional)
1 tablespoon olive oil
grated rind and juice of 1 lime

1 Heat the oil in a saucepan, add the onion and fry for 2–3 minutes until beginning to soften.

2 Add the lentils and stock and bring to the boil, then cover and simmer for 30–40 minutes until the lentils are tender and the stock has been absorbed. Add the tomatoes and spring onions and stir well.

3 Meanwhile, place the salsa ingredients in a liquidizer or food processor and blend for a few seconds until they are well combined but still retain a little texture.

4 Drizzle the salsa over the warm lentils and toss together. Serve with toasted chapattis or flat breads.

Fat 6 g
Carbohydrate 75 g
Protein 22 g
Energy 423 kcal (1747 kj)

Mixed leaf and pomegranate salad

Preparation time **10 minutes**
Serves **6**

3 tablespoons raspberry vinegar
2 tablespoons olive oil
1 pomegranate
125 g (4 oz) mixed salad leaves
   (such as baby spinach leaves, red
   mustard and mizuna)
salt and pepper
raspberries, to garnish (optional)

1 Put the raspberry vinegar, olive oil and a little salt and pepper into a salad bowl and mix lightly.

2 Cut the pomegranate in half, then break or cut it into large pieces and flex the skin so that the small red seeds fall out. Pick out any stubborn ones with a small knife and discard them. Add the remainder to the salad bowl, discarding the skin and pith.

3 Tear any large salad leaves into bite-sized pieces and toss them in the dressing. Sprinkle with the raspberries, if using, and serve immediately.

Fat 4 g
Carbohydrate 1 g
Protein 1 g
Energy 43 kcal (177 kj)

Warm courgette and lime salad

Preparation time **10 minutes**
Cooking time **10 minutes**
Serves **4**

1 tablespoon olive oil
grated rind and juice of 1 lime
1 garlic clove, finely chopped
2 tablespoons roughly chopped
    coriander leaves, plus extra
    to garnish
2 courgettes, about 325 g (11 oz)
    in total, cut into thin diagonal
    slices
salt and pepper

1 Mix together the oil, lime rind and juice, garlic, chopped coriander and salt and pepper in a plastic bag. Add the courgette slices and toss in the oil mixture. Seal and set aside until ready to cook.

2 Heat a ridged griddle. Arrange as many courgette slices as will fit in a single layer over the base of the pan and cook for 2–3 minutes until browned on the underside. Turn over the slices and brown on the other side. Transfer the slices to a warm serving dish while you cook the remaining courgettes in the same way.

3 Pour any remaining dressing over the courgettes, sprinkle with a little extra chopped coriander to garnish and serve immediately.

Fat 3 g
Carbohydrate 4 g
Protein 1 g
Energy 47 kcal (194 kj)

Honeyed figs with raspberries and goats' cheese

Preparation time **3 minutes**
Cooking time **3 minutes**
Serves **4–8**

8 fresh figs, preferably black
1 tablespoon clear honey
75 g (3 oz) low-fat goats' cheese,
    cut into 4 thin slices
125 g (4 oz) raspberries
a handful of flat leaf parsley,
    chopped, to garnish

1 Halve the figs, put them cut side up in a foil-lined grill pan and drizzle a little honey into the centre of each. Cook under a preheated hot grill for 2–3 minutes.

2 Serve the figs hot on individual plates with the goats' cheese and the raspberries, garnished with flat leaf parsley.

Fat 3 g
Carbohydrate 17 g
Protein 4 g
Energy 108 kcal (460 kj)

Fragrant cinnamon basmati rice

Preparation time **5 minutes**,
  plus soaking
Cooking time **18–20 minutes**
Serves **4**

250 g (8 oz) basmati rice
200 g (7 oz) peas
2 teaspoons cumin seeds
4 cinnamon sticks, each broken
  into 2–3 pieces
3 black cardamom pods
3 star anise
1 teaspoon salt
5 g (¼ oz) butter
500 ml (17 fl oz) water

1 Wash the rice in several changes of water, then soak for 2 hours in a large bowl in 1 litre (1¾ pints) water.

2 Drain the rice and put it in a large pan with all the other ingredients apart from the water. Pour in the measured water and cover the pan with a tightly fitting lid.

3 Cook the rice over a medium heat for 18–20 minutes, stirring gently halfway through cooking.

Fat 3 g
Carbohydrate 60 g
Protein 8 g
Energy 280 kcal (1195 kj)

Caramelized green beans

Preparation time **5 minutes**
Cooking time **12–15 minutes**
Serves **2**

2 teaspoons olive oil
1 garlic clove, crushed
200 g (7 oz) fine green beans,
  topped and tailed
1 tablespoon thyme leaves
3 tablespoons balsamic vinegar
2 tablespoons soy sauce, or salt
  to taste
¼ teaspoon black pepper
1 teaspoon sesame seeds,
  to garnish

1 Heat the oil in a nonstick frying pan or wok, add the garlic and beans and stir-fry over a medium heat for 2–3 minutes.

2 Stir in the thyme leaves, balsamic vinegar, soy sauce and black pepper. Cook for 10–12 minutes, until the beans are just cooked. Add a few tablespoons of hot water if the beans are beginning to stick to the base of the pan.

3 Serve the beans sprinkled with the sesame seeds.

Fat 4 g
Carbohydrate 5 g
Protein 4 g
Energy 74 kcal (307 kj)

Sweet potato and chilli mash

Preparation time **10 minutes**
Cooking time **15–20 minutes**
Serves **4**

3 sweet potatoes, about 875 g
  (1¾ lb) in total, chopped
5 g (¼ oz) butter
2 tablespoons semi-skimmed milk
15 g (½ oz) chives, snipped
1–2 tablespoons sweet chilli sauce

1 Put the sweet potatoes in a saucepan of water, bring to the boil and cook for 15–20 minutes or until soft. Drain the potatoes and return them to the saucepan.

2 Add the butter, milk, chives and chilli sauce and mash the potatoes thoroughly. Serve immediately.

Fat 2 g
Carbohydrate 47 g
Protein 3 g
Energy 205 kcal (874 kj)

Five-minute baby sweetcorn with coriander

Preparation time **5 minutes**
Cooking time **5 minutes**
Serves **4**

1 teaspoon whole coriander seeds
1 tablespoon olive oil
250 g (8 oz) baby sweetcorn cobs
good pinch of black pepper
2 teaspoons ground turmeric
30 g (1¼ oz) coriander leaves,
    finely chopped
2 tablespoons lemon juice

1 Lightly crush the coriander seeds with a rolling pin or using a pestle and mortar. Heat the oil in a nonstick frying pan or wok, add the coriander seeds and stir-fry for a few seconds.

2 Stir in the sweetcorn cobs with the black pepper and turmeric and cook for 3–4 minutes, then mix in the coriander leaves.

3 Add the lemon juice and allow it to sizzle in the pan just before serving.

Fat 3 g
Carbohydrate 2 g
Protein 2 g
Energy 48 kcal (198 kj)

Chilli and melon sorbet with melon and Serrano ham

Preparation time **35 minutes**,
  plus freezing
Serves **6**

1½ cantaloupe melons, quartered
  and deseeded
12 slices Serrano ham, prosciutto
  crudo or Parma ham

Chilli and melon sorbet
1 cantaloupe melon, halved, peeled
  and deseeded
2 tablespoons chopped mint
½–1 large red chilli, deseeded and
  finely chopped (to taste), plus
  chilli curls to decorate
1 egg white

1 Make the sorbet. Scoop the melon flesh into a liquidizer or food processor and blend until smooth. Stir in the chopped mint and add chilli to taste.

2 Transfer the mixture to an ice-cream maker and churn until thick. Alternatively, pour the mixture into a plastic box and freeze for 4 hours, beating once or twice to break up the ice crystals.

3 Mix in the egg white and continue churning until the sorbet is thick enough to scoop. If you are not serving it immediately, transfer the sorbet to a plastic box and store in the freezer. Otherwise, freeze for a minimum of 2 hours until firm.

4 Arrange the melon quarters and ham on 6 serving plates. Use warm spoons to scoop out the sorbet and put 2 spoonfuls of sorbet on top of each melon quarter. Decorate with red chilli curls and serve immediately.

Fat 6 g
Carbohydrate 7 g
Protein 11 g
Energy 125 kcal (525 kj)

Fish and seafood

Masala roast cod

Preparation time **15 minutes**
Cooking time **30 minutes**
Serves **4**

1 red chilli, chopped
2 garlic cloves, chopped
1 teaspoon minced fresh
   root ginger
1 teaspoon mustard seeds
large pinch of turmeric
2 cloves
2 cardamoms
5 peppercorns
3 tablespoons water
1 teaspoon olive oil
3 tablespoons low-fat yogurt
25 g (1 oz) breadcrumbs
500 g (1 lb) cod fillet
250 g (8 oz) ripe tomatoes,
   chopped
boiled rice, to serve

To garnish
lemon rind and wedges
lime wedges
coriander leaves

1 Put the chilli, garlic, ginger, mustard seeds, turmeric, cloves, cardamoms, peppercorns and measured water in a coffee grinder or blender and process to form a paste. Alternatively, use a pestle and mortar.

2 Heat the oil in a small nonstick saucepan and fry the chilli paste until the oil comes to the surface. Remove the pan from the heat and stir in the yogurt and breadcrumbs.

3 Place the cod in an ovenproof dish and spread the chilli paste over it. Scatter over the tomatoes, cover and cook in a preheated oven, 200°C (400 F), Gas Mark 6, for 30 minutes, or until the fish is tender.

4 Serve the cod with boiled rice sprinkled with coriander and strips of lemon rind, and garnish with wedges of lemon and lime for squeezing.

Fat 3 g
Carbohydrate 7 g
Protein 26 g
Energy 150 kcal (640 kj)

Seared skate wings with caper berries

Preparation time **5 minutes**
Cooking time **6–8 minutes**
Serves **4**

2 skate wings, about 300 g
  (10 oz) each
1 teaspoon olive oil
2 tablespoons capers, or caper
  berries with their stalks,
  halved lengthways
1 tablespoon grated lemon rind
2 tablespoons lemon juice
salt and pepper
lemon wedges, to garnish

1 Cut the skate wings in half, pat dry and brush each side with a little oil. Heat a griddle pan and sear the skate wings for 3 minutes on each side. If the wings are thick, cook them for a little longer.

2 Put the caper berries on top of the fish with the lemon rind and juice and cook for a few more seconds. Season to taste with salt and pepper and serve, garnished with lemon wedges.

Fat 1 g
Carbohydrate 0 g
Protein 23 g
Energy 105 kcal (446 kj)

Grilled sea bass with tomato sauce

Preparation time **15 minutes**
Cooking time **12–13 minutes**
Serves **6**

1 tablespoon olive oil
1 onion, finely chopped
300 g (10 oz) cherry tomatoes,
  halved
2 large pinches of saffron threads
  (optional)
150 ml (¼ pint) dry white wine
125 ml (4 fl oz) fish stock
grated rind of 1 lemon, the rest
  halved and thinly sliced
12 small sea bass fillets, about
  100 g (3½ oz) each, rinsed in
  cold water
1 teaspoon fennel seeds
salt and pepper
basil or oregano leaves, to garnish
  (optional)

1 Heat the oil in a nonstick frying pan, add the onion and fry for about 5 minutes or until softened and lightly browned. Add the tomatoes, the saffron if using, the wine and the stock and stir in the lemon rind. Season to taste with salt and pepper, then bring to the boil and cook for 2 minutes.

2 Pour the mixture into the base of a foil-lined grill pan, add the lemon slices and set aside until ready to complete.

3 Arrange the fish fillets, skin side up, on top of the tomato mixture. Use a teaspoon to scoop some of the saffron juices over the skin, then sprinkle with salt and pepper and the fennel seeds.

4 Cook the sea bass under a preheated grill for 5–6 minutes until the skin is crispy and the fish flakes easily when pressed with a knife. Transfer to serving plates and serve garnished with basil or oregano leaves, if using.

Fat 7 g
Carbohydrate 4 g
Protein 39 g
Energy 252 kcal (1057 kj)

Pan-fried halibut with papaya and coriander salsa

Preparation time **20 minutes**
Cooking time **10–12 minutes**
Serves **4**

2 teaspoons olive oil
3 garlic cloves, crushed
4 halibut steaks, about 600 g
    (1¼ lb) in total
watercress leaves, to serve
lime wedges, to garnish

Papaya and coriander salsa
1 papaya, cut into cubes
½ red onion, finely chopped
15 g (½ oz) coriander leaves,
    finely chopped
¼–½ teaspoon red chilli powder
1 red pepper, cored, deseeded and
    finely chopped
juice of ½ lime

1 Heat the oil in a large, nonstick frying pan. Add the garlic and stir for a few seconds. Put the fish steaks in the pan and fry for 10–12 minutes until just cooked, turning halfway through cooking.

2 Meanwhile, make the salsa by mixing together all the ingredients.

3 Serve the halibut steaks on a bed of watercress leaves, with the salsa and lime wedges on the side.

Fat 6 g
Carbohydrate 20 g
Protein 28 g
Energy 236 kcal (993 kj)

Plaice en papillotte with fennel and chilli

Preparation time **30 minutes**
Cooking time **8 minutes**
Serves **4**

1 fennel bulb, about 350 g
(11½ oz), finely chopped
2 red chillies, deseeded and
chopped
4 tablespoons lemon juice
2 teaspoons extra virgin olive oil
4 plaice fillets, about 675 g
(1 lb 6 oz) in total
1 small handful chopped dill
½ lemon, cut into wedges,
to garnish

Radicchio and orange salad
200 g (7 oz) red radicchio leaves
2 large oranges, peeled and
pith removed, separated
into segments

1 Put the fennel in a bowl with the chopped chillies. Add the lemon juice and olive oil and set aside.

2 Cut 4 sheets of baking parchment, each 35 x 18 cm (14 x 7 inches), and fold them in half widthways. Lay one half of a sheet over a plate and arrange a fish fillet to one side of the fold. Sprinkle over some chopped dill and fold over the paper to enclose the filling. Fold in the edges and pleat to secure. Repeat with the remaining fish.

3 Place the wrapped fish on a baking sheet and cook in a preheated oven, 220°C (425°F), Gas Mark 7, for about 8 minutes or until the baking parchment is puffed up and brown.

4 Make the salad. Combine the radicchio with the orange segments.

5 Place each fish parcel on a large plate and cut an X-shaped slit in the top or pull the paper apart to open the parcel, releasing a fragrant puff of steam, and curl back the paper.

6 Garnish with a lemon wedge and serve with individual bowls of the fennel and chilli mixture and of the radicchio and orange salad.

Fat 6 g
Carbohydrate 13 g
Protein 32 g
Energy 234 kcal (988 kJ)

Grilled sardines with tabbouleh

Preparation time **10 minutes**
Cooking time **15 minutes**
Serves **4**

125 g (4 oz) bulgar wheat
1 onion, finely chopped
2 ripe tomatoes, skinned and
    deseeded
1 tablespoon lemon juice
1 teaspoon grated lemon rind
small handful of mint leaves
4 small sardines, gutted and boned
salt and pepper

To garnish
lemon wedges
salad or herb leaves

1 Bring a small saucepan of water to the boil and add the bulgar wheat. Simmer for 5 minutes, then drain and refresh under cold water. Drain again and put into a bowl.

2 Meanwhile, dry-fry the onion for 5 minutes. Add the onion, tomatoes, lemon juice and rind to the bulgar wheat. Set aside 4 mint leaves and chop the remainder. Stir the chopped mint into the bulgar wheat mixture and season to taste with salt and pepper.

3 Open out each sardine and lay a mint leaf along the centre. Spoon over a little of the tabbouleh and carefully fold the fillet back over.

4 Grill the sardines for 5 minutes, then carefully turn them over and grill the other sides for 5 minutes more. Serve with the remaining tabbouleh (hot or cold), garnished with lemon wedges and a few salad or herb leaves.

Fat 5 g
Carbohydrate 27 g
Protein 14 g
Energy 209 kcal (877 kj)

Griddled tuna with shallot jus

Preparation time **5 minutes**
Cooking time **15 minutes**
Serves **4**

4 tuna steaks, about 100 g
 (3½ oz) each
flat leaf parsley sprigs, to garnish

Sauce
4 shallots, finely chopped
300 ml (½ pint) red wine
150 ml (¼ pint) Marsala
salt and pepper

1 Heat a griddle or frying pan until it is very hot. Cook the tuna steaks, 2 at a time, for 3 minutes on each side. Remove the steaks from the pan and keep warm.

2 Make the shallot jus. Mix the shallots, red wine and Marsala in a saucepan, season with salt and pepper and boil rapidly until the sauce is reduced by half. Return the tuna steaks to the frying pan, add the sauce and simmer for 2 minutes. Serve immediately, garnished with parsley sprigs.

Fat 5 g
Carbohydrate 4 g
Protein 24 g
Energy 240 kcal (1000 kj)

Thai-style monkfish and mushroom kebabs

Preparation time **15 minutes**,
  plus marinating
Cooking time **10 minutes**
Serves **4**

500–750 g (1–1½ lb) monkfish
  tails, skinned
1 onion, quartered and layers
  separated
8 mushrooms
1 courgette, cut into 8 pieces
vegetable oil, for brushing
watercress or flat leaf parsley,
  to garnish

Marinade
grated rind and juice of 2 limes
1 garlic clove, finely chopped
2 tablespoons finely sliced fresh
  root ginger
2 chillies, red or green or
  1 of each, deseeded and
  finely chopped
2 lemon grass stalks,
  finely chopped
handful of chopped coriander
1 glass of red wine
2 tablespoons sesame oil
pepper

1 Make the marinade by combining all the ingredients in a large bowl. Cut the fish into large cubes and add to the marinade with the onion, mushrooms and courgette. Cover and refrigerate for 1 hour to allow the flavours to blend.

2 Lightly brush the rack of a grill pan with oil to prevent the kebabs from sticking. Thread 4 skewers alternately with pieces of fish, mushrooms, courgette and onion. Brush with a little oil and grill under a preheated hot grill for about 10 minutes, turning them at intervals. Serve immediately, garnished with watercress or flat leaf parsley.

Fat 6 g
Carbohydrate 4 g
Protein 25 g
Energy 185 kcal (780 kj)

Lemon grass fish skewers

Preparation time **10–15 minutes**
Cooking time **4–5 minutes**
Serves **4**

500 g (1 lb) skinless haddock
  fillets, chopped
1 tablespoon chopped mint
2 tablespoons chopped coriander
2 teaspoons red Thai curry paste
2 lime leaves, finely chopped,
  or the grated rind of 1 lime
2 lemon grass stalks, quartered
  lengthways
vegetable oil, for brushing

To serve
sweet chilli sauce
lime wedges

1 Put the fish, mint, coriander, curry paste and lime leaves or rind in a liquidizer or food processor and blend for 30 seconds until well combined.

2 Divide the mixture into 8 portions, then form each around a lemon grass stalk 'skewer'.

3 Brush the skewers with a little oil, place under a preheated hot grill and cook for 4–5 minutes until cooked through. Serve with a little sweet chilli sauce and lime wedges.

Fat 3 g
Carbohydrate 0 g
Protein 19 g
Energy 106 kcal (438 kj)

Kerala prawn curry

Preparation time **5 minutes**
Cooking time **8 minutes**
Serves **4**

500 g (I lb) large cooked peeled
  prawns
½ teaspoon ground turmeric
1 teaspoon vegetable oil
1 red onion, cut into fine wedges
2 green chillies, deseeded
  and sliced
10 curry leaves (optional)
100 ml (3½ fl oz) coconut milk
2 tablespoons lime juice
a few coriander leaves
salt and pepper

1 Put the prawns in a bowl, sprinkle with the turmeric and set aside.

2 Heat the oil in a nonstick frying pan or wok and stir-fry the onion wedges and chillies until softened. Add the prawns, curry leaves, if using, and coconut milk. Simmer for 5 minutes.

3 Sprinkle over the lime juice and season to taste with salt and pepper. Scatter with coriander leaves and stir once. Serve immediately.

Fat 3 g
Carbohydrate 4 g
Protein 29 g
Energy 159 kcal (670 kj)

Wild rice jambalaya

Preparation time **15 minutes**
Cooking time **35 minutes**
Serves **4**

125 g (4 oz) wild rice
1 teaspoon olive oil
50 g (2 oz) celery, chopped
½ red pepper, cored, deseeded
  and diced
½ green or yellow pepper, cored,
  deseeded and diced
1 onion, chopped
1 rasher of rindless lean back
  bacon, trimmed of fat and diced
2 garlic cloves, crushed
2 tablespoons tomato purée
1 tablespoon chopped thyme
125 g (4 oz) long-grain rice
1 green chilli, deseeded and
  finely chopped
½ teaspoon cayenne pepper
1 tablespoon chopped canned
  pimientos (optional)
400 g (13 oz) can tomatoes,
  drained
300 ml (½ pint) chicken stock
150 ml (¼ pint) dry white wine
250 g (8 oz) raw prawns
3 tablespoons chopped coriander
  or parsley, to garnish

1 Put the wild rice in a saucepan with sufficient water to cover. Bring to the boil and boil for 5 minutes. Remove the pan from the heat and cover tightly. Leave the rice to steam for about 10 minutes until the grains are tender. Drain.

2 Heat the oil in a large, nonstick frying pan. Add the celery, peppers, onion, bacon and garlic and cook, stirring, for 3–4 minutes until the vegetables are soft. Stir in the tomato purée and thyme. Cook for another 2 minutes.

3 Add the wild rice, long-grain rice, chilli, cayenne pepper, pimientos if using, tomatoes, stock and wine to the pan. Bring to the boil, then reduce the heat and simmer for 10 minutes until the rice is tender but still firm to the bite.

4 Add the prawns and cook, stirring occasionally, for 5 minutes, until the prawns have turned opaque. Spoon the jambalaya into large warm bowls, scatter with coriander or parsley and serve.

Fat 3 g
Carbohydrate 60 g
Protein 20 g
Energy 378 kcal (1586 kj)

Zarzuela with mussels, calamari and cod

Preparation time **30 minutes**
Cooking time **24 minutes**
Serves **4**

1 tablespoon olive oil
1 large onion, finely chopped
2 garlic cloves, finely chopped
½ teaspoon pimentón
  (smoked paprika)
500 g (1 lb) tomatoes, skinned
  and chopped
1 red pepper, cored, deseeded
  and diced
200 ml (7 fl oz) fish stock
150 ml (¼ pint) dry white wine
2 large pinches of saffron threads
4 small bay leaves
500 g (1 lb) fresh mussels, soaked
  in cold water
200 g (7 oz) cleaned calamari,
  rinsed in cold water
375 g (12 oz) cod loin, skinned
salt and pepper

1 Heat the oil in a large, nonstick frying pan. Add the onion and fry for 5 minutes until softened and just beginning to brown. Stir in the garlic and pimentón and cook for 1 minute.

2 Mix in the tomatoes, red pepper, stock, wine and saffron. Add the bay leaves, season to taste with salt and pepper and bring to the boil. Cover the pan and simmer gently for 10 minutes. Set aside until needed.

3 Discard any mussels that are open or cracked. Scrub the shells with a nailbrush, remove any barnacles and pull off the hairy beard. Return the mussels to a bowl of clean water. Separate the calamari tubes from the tentacles and slice the tubes. Cut the cod into cubes.

4 Reheat the tomato sauce if necessary, add the cod and the calamari slices and cook for 2 minutes. Add the mussels, cover and cook for 4 minutes. Add the calamari tentacles and cook for 2 minutes until cooked through and all the mussels have opened (discard any that remain closed). Gently stir the stew and spoon into bowls to serve.

Fat 5 g
Carbohydrate 11 g
Protein 32 g
Energy 240 kcal (1009 kj)

Prawns with piri-piri

Preparation time **15 minutes**,
plus chilling
Cooking time **5–6 minutes**
Serves **6**

3 tablespoons olive oil
grated rind and juice of 1 lemon
2 teaspoons piri-piri seasoning
2 teaspoons tomato purée
2 garlic cloves, finely chopped
400 g (13 oz) raw, headless tiger
  prawns (not shelled, and thawed
  if frozen)
salt and pepper

To garnish
chopped parsley
lemon wedges

1 Mix the oil, lemon rind and juice, piri-piri seasoning, tomato purée and garlic in a shallow bowl with a little salt and pepper.

2 Put the prawns in a sieve, rinse under cold running water and drain well. Add the prawns to the piri-piri mixture and toss until evenly coated. Cover and chill for at least 2 hours.

3 Thread the prawns on to 12 skewers through the thickest part of the body and tail and arrange them on a foil-lined grill rack.

4 Cook the prawns under a preheated grill for 5–6 minutes, turning them once, until they are bright pink. Arrange on a serving plate, and serve, sprinkled with chopped parsley and garnished with lemon wedges.

Fat 6 g
Carbohydrate 1 g
Protein 12 g
Energy 104 kcal (433 kj)

Catalan mussels

Preparation time **10 minutes**
Cooking time **15 minutes**
Serves **4**

1 tablespoon olive oil
1 onion, finely chopped
2 garlic cloves, crushed
1 red chilli, deseeded and
    finely chopped
pinch of paprika
400 g (13 oz) can chopped
    tomatoes
1 kg (2 lb) mussels
salt and pepper
chopped parsley, to garnish

1 Heat the oil in a large, nonstick frying pan or wok. Fry the onion, garlic, chilli and paprika over a medium heat for 10 minutes or until soft. Stir in the tomatoes and season with salt and pepper. Cover and simmer over a low heat while you clean the mussels.

2 Discard any mussels that are open or cracked. Scrub the shells with a nailbrush, remove any barnacles, pull off the hairy beards and return the mussels to a bowl of clean water. Stir the mussels into the tomato sauce, increase the temperature and cover with a lid. Cook for 5 minutes until the shells have opened. (Discard any mussels that remain closed.)

3 Pile the mussels into warmed serving bowls, sprinkle with chopped parsley and serve at once.

Fat 4 g
Carbohydrate 6 g
Protein 15 g
Energy 119 kcal (498 kj)

Pan-fried scallops with white bean purée and leeks

Preparation time **10 minutes**
Cooking time **about 15 minutes**
Serves **4**

2 x 400 g (13 oz) cans cannellini
    beans, drained and rinsed
2 garlic cloves
200 ml (7 fl oz) vegetable stock
2 tablespoons chopped parsley
2 teaspoons olive oil
16 baby leeks
3 tablespoons water
16 large scallops, shelled
    and prepared
parsley sprigs, to garnish

1 Place the beans, garlic and stock in a saucepan, bring to the boil and simmer for 10 minutes. Remove the pan from the heat and drain off any excess liquid. Mash the beans with a potato masher and stir in the parsley. Keep warm.

2 Heat half the oil in a nonstick frying pan, add the leeks and fry for 2 minutes. Add the measured water, cover and simmer for 5–6 minutes until tender.

3 Meanwhile, heat the remaining oil in a small frying pan, add the scallops and fry for 1 minute on each side. Serve the scallops with the bean purée and leeks, garnished with parsley sprigs.

Fat 4 g
Carbohydrate 27 g
Protein 37 g
Energy 293 kcal (1210 kj)

Meat, poultry
and game

Peppered beef with horseradish-dressed leaves

Preparation time **20 minutes**
Cooking time **3–7 minutes**
Serves **6**

2 thick-cut sirloin steaks, about
    500 g (1 lb) in total
3 teaspoons coloured peppercorns,
    coarsely crushed
coarse salt flakes
200 g (7 oz) low-fat natural yogurt
1–1½ teaspoons horseradish sauce
    (to taste)
1 garlic clove, crushed
150 g (5 oz) mixed green salad
    leaves
100 g (3½ oz) button mushrooms,
    sliced
1 red onion, thinly sliced
1 tablespoon olive oil
salt and pepper

1 Trim the fat from the steaks and rub the meat with the crushed peppercorns and salt flakes.

2 Mix together the yogurt, horseradish sauce and garlic and season to taste with salt and pepper. Add the salad leaves, mushrooms and most of the red onion and toss gently.

3 Heat the oil in a large, nonstick frying pan, add the steaks and cook over a high heat for 2 minutes until browned. Turn over and cook for a further 2 minutes for medium rare, 3–4 minutes for medium or 5 minutes for well done.

4 Spoon the salad leaves into the centre of 6 serving plates. Thinly slice the steaks and arrange the pieces on top. Serve garnished with the remaining red onion.

Fat 6 g
Carbohydrate 4 g
Protein 19 g
Energy 148 kcal (620 kj)

Green peppercorn steak

Preparation time **5 minutes**
Cooking time **6–8 minutes**
Serves **4**

4 lean fillet steaks, about 75 g
  (3 oz) each
1 tablespoon green peppercorns
  in brine, drained
2 tablespoons light soy sauce
1 teaspoon balsamic vinegar
8 cherry tomatoes, halved
thyme sprigs, to garnish

1 Heat a griddle pan until it is very hot. Cook the steaks for 2–3 minutes on each side, then remove them from the pan and keep hot.

2 Add the peppercorns, soy sauce, balsamic vinegar and cherry tomatoes to the pan. Allow the liquids to sizzle for 2 minutes or until the tomatoes are soft. Spoon the sauce over the steaks and garnish with thyme sprigs.

Fat 5 g
Carbohydrate 4 g
Protein 17 g
Energy 130 kcal (548 kj)

Russian meatballs

Preparation time **15 minutes**,
    plus chilling
Cooking time **45 minutes**
Serves **4**

375 g (12 oz) lean minced beef
1 onion, roughly chopped
1 tablespoon tomato purée
1 teaspoon dried mixed herbs
salt and pepper
chopped parsley and parsley sprigs,
    to garnish
paprika, to sprinkle

Tomato sauce
1 red onion, finely chopped
400 g (13 oz) can chopped
    tomatoes
pinch of paprika
1 teaspoon dried mixed herbs

1 Put the meat, onion, tomato purée and dried mixed herbs in a liquidizer or food processor. Season well with salt and pepper and blend until smooth. Shape the mixture into 12 balls and chill them in the refrigerator for 30 minutes.

2 Meanwhile, put all the sauce ingredients into a saucepan and cook, uncovered, over a low heat for 15–20 minutes, stirring occasionally.

3 Season the sauce to taste with salt and pepper and transfer to an ovenproof dish. Arrange the meatballs on top and cook in a preheated oven, 180°C (350°F), Gas Mark 4, for 45 minutes. Serve the meatballs sprinkled with chopped parsley and paprika and garnished with parsley sprigs.

Fat 5 g
Carbohydrate 8 g
Protein 21 g
Energy 154 kcal (650 kj)

Green beef curry

Preparation time **5 minutes**
Cooking time **about 10 minutes**
Serves **4**

300 g (l0 oz) lean beef fillet,
  finely sliced
1 red onion, cut into thin wedges
1–2 tablespoons Thai green
  curry paste
125 g (4 oz) mangetout, thinly
  sliced lengthways
150 ml (¼ pint) water
small bunch of basil leaves

1 Heat a large, nonstick frying pan or wok. Dry-fry the beef for 2 minutes and remove with a slotted spoon, leaving the juices in the pan.

2 Reheat the pan and stir-fry the onion for 1 minute until softened. Add the curry paste and stir-fry for another minute or so. Add the mangetout and measured water.

3 Return the meat to the pan and stir-fry for a further 5 minutes. When the beef has cooked, add the basil and stir-fry for 30 seconds. Serve immediately.

Fat 5 g
Carbohydrate 4 g
Protein 17 g
Energy 128 kcal (536 kj)

Carnival chicken with sweet potato mash

Preparation time **15–20 minutes**, plus marinating
Cooking time **20 minutes**
Serves **4**

4 skinless chicken breasts, about
    150 g (5 oz) each
flat leaf parsley sprigs, to garnish

Marinade
100 ml (3½ fl oz) sweet sherry
1 teaspoon Angostura bitters
1 tablespoon light soy sauce
1 tablespoon chopped fresh
    root ginger
pinch of ground cumin
pinch of ground coriander
1 teaspoon dried mixed herbs
1 small onion, finely chopped
75 ml (3 fl oz) chicken stock

Sweet potato mash
2 sweet potatoes
2 tablespoons low-fat fromage
    frais (optional)
salt and pepper

1 Place the chicken breasts in a non-metallic dish. In a bowl mix together all the ingredients for the marinade and spoon it over the chicken, making sure that the pieces are well coated. Cover and leave to marinate in the refrigerator overnight.

2 Arrange the chicken on a grill pan and cook under a preheated medium grill for 20 minutes, turning over the pieces halfway through cooking.

3 Meanwhile, boil the sweet potatoes in their skins for 20 minutes until soft. Drain well and peel. Mash the potato and allow to dry off a bit then stir in the fromage frais, if using. Season with salt and pepper and serve with the chicken, garnished with flat leaf parsley sprigs.

Fat 5 g
Carbohydrate 26 g
Protein 36 g
Energy 315 kcal (1332 kj)

Chicken curry with baby spinach

Preparation time **10 minutes**
Cooking time **25 minutes**
Serves **4**

1 tablespoon vegetable oil
4 boneless, skinless chicken
    breasts, about 125 g (4 oz) each,
    halved lengthways
1 onion, sliced
2 garlic cloves, chopped
1 green chilli, chopped
4 cardamom pods, lightly crushed
1 teaspoon cumin seeds
1 teaspoon dried chilli flakes
1 teaspoon ground ginger
1 teaspoon ground turmeric
250 g (8 oz) baby spinach leaves
300 g (10 oz) tomatoes, chopped
150 ml (¼ pint) low-fat
    Greek yogurt
2 tablespoons chopped coriander
coriander sprigs, to garnish

1 Heat the oil in a large, nonstick frying pan or wok. Add the chicken, onion, garlic and chilli and fry for 4–5 minutes or until the chicken begins to brown and the onion to soften.

2 Add the cardamom pods, cumin seeds, chilli flakes, ginger and turmeric and continue to fry for 1 minute.

3 Add the spinach to the pan, cover and cook gently until the spinach wilts, then stir in the tomatoes and simmer for 15 minutes, removing the lid for the last 5 minutes of cooking.

4 Stir the yogurt and coriander into the curry and garnish with coriander sprigs before serving.

Fat 6 g
Carbohydrate 10 g
Protein 27 g
Energy 205 kcal (847 kj)

Chicken breasts with Puy lentil and watercress stuffing

Preparation time **15 minutes**
Cooking time **55 minutes**
Serves **4**

50 g (2 oz) watercress
50 g (2 oz) Puy lentils, cooked
50 g (2 oz) very low-fat cream
   cheese or fromage frais
1 onion, grated
1 teaspoon grated lemon rind
50 g (2 oz) chestnut mushrooms,
   finely chopped
4 skinless chicken breasts, about
   150 g (5 oz) each
1 large potato, parboiled

1 Place the watercress and cooked Puy lentils in a blender or food processor with the cream cheese or fromage frais and blend until smooth. Season well with salt and pepper, then transfer to a bowl.

2 Dry-fry the grated onion for 5 minutes until soft and slightly coloured. Add the lemon rind and the mushrooms and fry for a further 5 minutes to extract the juice from the mushrooms. Stir the onions and mushrooms into the watercress and lentil mixture.

3 Make a deep cut along the length of each chicken breast, opening up the slit to form a pocket. Spoon a little of the stuffing into each pocket.

4 Finely slice the potato and arrange a quarter of the slices in a row in an ovenproof dish, making sure the slices overlap slightly. Lift a chicken breast on to the potatoes. Repeat with the remaining potato and the other three chicken breasts. Season with pepper. Bake in a preheated oven, 190°C (375°F), Gas Mark 5, for 45 minutes, covering the dish with foil if necessary to prevent the chicken from over-browning.

Fat 5 g
Carbohydrate 12 g
Protein 37 g
Energy 238 kcal (1002 kj)

Seriously hot jerk chicken with sweet potato wedges

Preparation time **20 minutes**
Cooking time **50 minutes**
Serves **4**

4 boneless, skinless chicken
    breasts, about 125 g (4 oz) each

Jerk seasoning
8–10 allspice berries
2 spring onions, green part only,
    sliced
4 garlic cloves, crushed
1 cm (½ inch) fresh root ginger,
    peeled and shredded
pinch of finely grated nutmeg
2 pinches of ground cinnamon
1 teaspoon thyme leaves
1–2 Scotch Bonnet chillies,
    deseeded and finely chopped
2 tablespoons soy sauce
juice of 2 limes

Sweet potato wedges
2 orange-fleshed sweet potatoes,
    about 750 g (1½ lb) in total,
    unpeeled
1 tablespoon olive oil
2 tablespoons chopped parsley
2 tablespoons chopped chives

1 Make the jerk seasoning. Crush the allspice berries using a pestle and mortar or in a blender. Add the spring onions and pound until well mixed. Add the garlic, ginger, nutmeg, cinnamon, thyme leaves and chillies. Stir in the soy sauce and lime juice and mix well. If necessary, add a little water to bind.

2 Score the chicken breasts on both sides and rub in the jerk seasoning. Bake the chicken in a preheated oven, 190°C (375°F), Gas Mark 5, for 30–40 minutes or until it is crusty on the outside.

3 Meanwhile, put the sweet potatoes in a saucepan of cold water and bring to the boil. Cook the potatoes for 8–10 minutes until parboiled, drain and leave to cool. Remove the skins and cut the potatoes into wedges.

4 Heat the oil in a large, nonstick frying pan and fry the potato wedges for about 10 minutes until they are coloured on both sides. Sprinkle with the parsley and chives and serve with the cooked chicken cut into thick slices.

Fat 7 g
Carbohydrate 40 g
Protein 31 g
Energy 343 kcal (1452 kj)

Blackened chicken skewers

Preparation time **5 minutes**,
   plus marinating
Cooking time **20 minutes**
Serves **4**

300 g (10 oz) boneless, skinless
   chicken breast, diced
1 tablespoon Cajun seasoning mix
2 tablespoons lemon juice
1 teaspoon olive oil
coriander sprigs, to garnish

1 Place the chicken in a bowl and add the seasoning mix, lemon juice and olive oil. Toss well and leave to marinate for 15 minutes. Meanwhile, soak 8 wooden skewers in warm water.

2 Drain the skewers and thread the pieces of chicken on to them. Cover the ends of the skewers with foil, place under a preheated medium grill and cook for 20 minutes, turning them halfway through cooking. When the chicken is cooked through, lift the skewers from the grill and reserve any juices.

3 Remove the chicken from the skewers and garnish with coriander sprigs. Serve with the juices and, if liked, a timbale of boiled rice and a green salad.

Fat 3 g
Carbohydrate 0 g
Protein 16 g
Energy 94 kcal (397 kj)

Pan-fried chicken livers with fennel

Preparation time **5 minutes**
Cooking time **10–12 minutes**
Serves **4**

1 tablespoon plain flour
225 g (7½ oz) chicken livers
2 teaspoons olive oil
225 g (7½ oz) fennel bulb and
   leaves, sliced
3 tablespoons chopped flat
   leaf parsley
2 tablespoons lemon juice
salt and pepper
watercress leaves, to serve

1 Mix the flour with a little salt and pepper and use the seasoned flour to coat the chicken livers.

2 Heat the oil in a large, nonstick frying pan and stir-fry the fennel over a moderately high heat for 3 minutes.

3 Add the seasoned liver to the pan and cook, stirring gently, over a moderately high heat for 5–8 minutes. Slowly mix in the parsley. Pour in the lemon juice, which will make a sizzling sound, remove the pan from the heat and serve the liver immediately on a bed of watercress leaves.

Fat 5 g
Carbohydrate 6 g
Protein 12 g
Energy 115 kcal (483 kj)

Thai chicken shells with coriander and coconut rice

Preparation time **10 minutes**
Cooking time **about 15 minutes**
Serves **4**

1 teaspoon oil
2 chicken breasts, about 150 g
    (5 oz) each, sliced
1 tablespoon red or green Thai
    curry paste
400 ml (14 fl oz) can coconut milk
250 g (8 oz) basmati rice
100 ml (3½ fl oz) water
3 tablespoons chopped coriander

To serve
3 spring onions, sliced
2 Little Gem lettuces, separated
    into individual leaves, hearts
    reserved
2 limes, cut into wedges

1 Heat the oil in a large, nonstick frying pan, add the chicken and fry for 2 minutes.

2 Add the curry paste and continue to fry for 1 minute, then add half the coconut milk, bring to the boil and simmer gently for 10 minutes.

3 Meanwhile, place the rice in a saucepan with the remaining coconut milk and the measured water. Bring to the boil, cover and simmer for 10–12 minutes until the liquid is absorbed, adding a little extra water if necessary. Stir through the coriander.

4 Arrange a little chicken, spring onion and rice on the larger lettuce leaves and squeeze the lime wedges over the filled shells before serving.

Fat 6 g
Carbohydrate 33 g
Protein 18 g
Energy 276 kcal (1139 kj)

Tea-infused duck with flamed pak choi salad

Preparation time **25 minutes**,
    plus chilling
Cooking time **10 minutes**
Serves **6**

3 teaspoons green tea
    (or 3 teabags)
250 ml (8 fl oz) boiling water
3 duck breasts, about 150 g
    (5 oz) each
3 tablespoons soy sauce
250 g (8 oz) carrots, cut into
    matchstick strips
4 small pak choi, about 400 g
    (13 oz) in total, leaves and
    stems thickly sliced but
    kept separate
3 spring onions, sliced
2 tablespoons orange liqueur
juice of 1 orange

1 Make the tea with the measured boiling water and leave to infuse for 5 minutes. Strain and leave to cool.

2 Make crisscross cuts in the duck skin and put the duck, skin side up, in a shallow non-metallic dish. Pour the tea over the duck breasts, cover and chill for 3–4 hours or overnight.

3 Put the duck breasts in a nonstick roasting tin, drizzle 1 tablespoon of the soy sauce over the skin and roast in a preheated oven, 220°C (425°F), Gas Mark 7, for 10 minutes until the skin is crispy but the meat is still slightly pink. After 5 minutes transfer 2 teaspoons of fat from the roasting tin to a large, nonstick frying pan or wok. Reheat the fat, add the carrot sticks and stir-fry for 2 minutes.

4 Add the pak choi stems to the carrots and cook for 1 minute. Add the pak choi leaves, spring onions and remaining soy sauce and cook for 30 seconds. Pour on the liqueur, light with a long taper and stand well back. When the flames subside, pour in the orange juice and warm through. Lift out the duck breasts with a slotted spoon and slice thinly.

5 To serve, spoon the vegetables into 6 small dishes and top with slices of duck breast.

Fat 4 g
Carbohydrate 9 g
Protein 18 g
Energy 148 kcal (620 kj)

Venison casserole

Preparation time **15 minutes**
Cooking time **2 hours**
Serves **4**

2 onions, sliced
4 venison steaks, about 125 g
  (4 oz) each
1 bouquet garni
½ cinnamon stick
5 pickled walnuts, sliced
250 ml (8 fl oz) beef stock
3 tablespoons red wine
1 teaspoon Angostura bitters
4 large field or portobello
  mushrooms
2 tablespoons chopped parsley,
  to garnish

1 Put the onions in an ovenproof casserole and lay the venison steaks on top. Add the bouquet garni, cinnamon stick and pickled walnuts. Pour over the stock, wine and Angostura bitters and cover. Cook in a preheated oven, 180°C (350°F), Gas Mark 4, for 1¾ hours until the meat is tender.

2 Remove the stalks from the mushrooms and wipe the caps clean. Add the whole mushroom caps to the casserole, covering them partially with the juices. Return the casserole to the oven for an additional 15 minutes.

3 Place a mushroom on each plate and top with a venison steak. Spoon the meat juices and onions on top and serve sprinkled with chopped parsley.

Fat 7 g
Carbohydrate 6 g
Protein 30 g
Energy 225 kcal (946 kj)

Herby rabbit casserole

Preparation time **10 minutes**
Cooking time **1 hour 10 minutes**
Serves **4**

375 g (12 oz) lean rabbit meat,
   diced
1 tablespoon chopped rosemary,
   plus 1 sprig to garnish
1 tablespoon dried mixed herbs
1 tablespoon plain flour
1 teaspoon olive oil
1 red onion, cut into wedges
1 piece of orange peel
4 sun-dried tomatoes, rehydrated
   and chopped
150 ml (¼ pint) red wine
50 g (2 oz) Puy lentils
salt and pepper

1 Put the meat in a large polythene bag, add the chopped rosemary and mixed herbs and flour and shake well to coat the meat.

2 Heat the oil in a large, flameproof casserole. Fry the coated meat for a few minutes until browned. Add the onion wedges, orange peel and tomatoes.

3 Pour the wine into the casserole and add enough water to just cover the meat. Season well with salt and pepper. Cover the casserole and simmer for 40 minutes– 1 hour or until the meat is tender and the vegetables are cooked.

4 About 30 minutes before the end of cooking time, rinse the lentils and cook in a saucepan of boiling water for 20 minutes. Drain the lentils and stir them into the casserole. Simmer for 10 minutes. Remove the orange peel before serving and garnish the rabbit with a rosemary sprig.

Fat 5 g
Carbohydrate 13 g
Protein 25 g
Energy 218 kcal (917 kj)

Turkey ragout

Preparation time **10 minutes**
Cooking time **1 hour 50 minutes**
Serves **4**

1 turkey drumstick, about
   625 g (1¼ lb)
2 garlic cloves
15 baby onions or shallots
3 carrots, diagonally sliced
300 ml (½ pint) red wine
few thyme sprigs
2 bay leaves
2 tablespoons chopped flat
   leaf parsley
1 teaspoon port wine jelly
1 teaspoon wholegrain mustard
salt and pepper

1 Carefully remove the skin from the turkey drumstick and make a few cuts in the flesh. Finely slice 1 garlic clove and push the slivers into the slashes.

2 Crush the remaining garlic clove. Transfer the drumstick to a large, flameproof casserole or roasting tin with the onions, carrots, crushed garlic, red wine, thyme and bay leaves. Season well with salt and pepper, cover and cook in a preheated oven, 180°C (350°F), Gas Mark 4, for about 1¾ hours.

3 Remove the turkey and vegetables from the casserole and keep hot. Bring the sauce to the boil on the hob, discarding the bay leaves. Add the parsley, port wine jelly and mustard. Boil for 5 minutes, until slightly thickened. Check and adjust the seasoning. Carve the turkey and serve with the juices.

Fat 4 g
Carbohydrate 7 g
Protein 20 g
Energy 190 kcal (800 kj)

Vegetarian

Spaghetti with mixed herb dressing

Preparation time **5 minutes**
Cooking time **12 minutes**
Serves **4**

300 g (10 oz) dried angel
   hair spaghetti

Mixed herb dressing
2 tablespoons chopped
   oregano leaves
2 tablespoons chopped flat
   leaf parsley
2 tablespoons balsamic vinegar
2 tablespoons red wine vinegar
2 tablespoons orange juice
1 small garlic clove, crushed
1 tablespoon olive oil
salt and pepper

1 Bring a large saucepan of salted water to the boil. Cook the pasta for 12 minutes or according to the instructions on the packet.

2 Meanwhile, make the dressing. Put all ingredients in a small saucepan, season lightly with salt and pepper and bring to the boil. Remove the pan from the heat and leave the dressing to infuse for 5 minutes.

3 Drain the pasta and return it to the saucepan. Pour the dressing over the pasta and toss to combine. Serve immediately.

Fat 4 g
Carbohydrate 57 g
Protein 9 g
Energy 287 kcal (1217 kj)

Mushroom crêpes

Preparation time **20–25 minutes**
Cooking time **35 minutes**
Serves **4**

50 g (2 oz) plain flour
150 ml (¼ pint) skimmed milk
1 small egg, beaten
1 teaspoon olive oil
salt and pepper
flat leaf parsley sprigs, to garnish

Filling
300 g (10 oz) chestnut mushrooms,
   chopped
1 bunch of spring onions, finely
   chopped
1 garlic clove, chopped
400 g (13 oz) can chopped
   tomatoes, drained
2 tablespoons chopped oregano

1 Make the crêpe batter. Put the flour, milk, egg and salt and pepper in a liquidizer or food processor and blend until smooth or whisk by hand.

2 Heat a few drops of oil in a nonstick frying pan. Pour in a ladleful of batter and cook for 1 minute. Carefully flip the pancake and cook the other side. Slide the pancake out of the pan on to greaseproof paper. Make 3 more pancakes in the same way, adding a few more drops of oil to the pan between each one, and stack the pancakes between sheets of greaseproof paper.

3 Make the filling. Put all the ingredients in a small saucepan and cook, stirring occasionally, for 5 minutes. Divide the filling among the pancakes, reserving a little of the mixture to serve, and roll them up.

4 Transfer the pancakes to an ovenproof dish and cook in a preheated oven, 180°C (350°F), Gas Mark 4, for 20 minutes. Serve with the remaining mushroom mixture and garnish with parsley sprigs.

Fat 3 g
Carbohydrate 15 g
Protein 7 g
Energy 112 kcal (470 kj)

Speedy kidney bean and coriander curry

Preparation time **5 minutes**
Cooking time **10 minutes**
Serves **4**

2 teaspoons corn oil
1 teaspoon cumin seeds
1 tablespoon tomato purée
2 teaspoons curry powder
1 teaspoon ground turmeric
1 teaspoon ground coriander
1 teaspoon ground cumin
2 teaspoons garam masala
410 g (13¼ oz) can kidney
   beans, drained
2 spring onions, sliced
2 tablespoons chopped
   coriander leaves
salt
mixed salad leaves or pitta breads,
   to serve

1 Heat the oil in a nonstick frying pan. Add the cumin seeds and let them pop for a few seconds.

2 Stir the tomato purée, curry powder, ground spices and garam masala into the pan and blend well together over a low heat.

3 Mix in the kidney beans, spring onions and coriander leaves. Add salt to taste and stir in a few tablespoons of hot water if you prefer more sauce. Serve the curry hot with mixed salad leaves or in warmed pitta breads.

Fat 3 g
Carbohydrate 21 g
Protein 8 g
Energy 136 kcal (572 kj)

Vietnamese vegetable rolls with plum and wasabi sauce

Preparation time **30 minutes**
Cooking time **10–15 minutes**
Serves **4**

200 g (7 oz) pak choi
2 tablespoons sunflower oil
100 g (3½ oz) sweet potato, cut
    into matchstick strips
100 g (3½ oz) carrot, cut into
    matchstick strips
½ bunch of spring onions, cut into
    matchstick strips
50 g (2 oz) bean sprouts, rinsed
    and drained
2 garlic cloves, finely chopped
2 cm (¾ inch) fresh root ginger,
    peeled and finely chopped
8 rice pancakes
bunch of coriander

Plum and wasabi sauce

4 ripe red plums, about 250 g
    (8 oz) in total, stoned and
    chopped
2 tablespoons water
1 tablespoon soy sauce
wasabi sauce (Japanese mustard),
    to taste
1 tablespoon caster sugar

1 Cut the leaves from the pak choi and slice the stems into matchstick strips. Heat 1 tablespoon of the oil in a large, nonstick frying pan or wok, add the sweet potato and carrot and stir-fry for 2 minutes. Add the spring onions and pak choi stems and cook for 1 minute. Mix in the bean sprouts, garlic and ginger and cook for 1 minute. Transfer to a bowl.

2 Heat the remaining oil in the pan, add the pak choi leaves and cook for 2–3 minutes until just wilted.

3 Dip a rice pancake into a bowl of hot water and leave for 20–30 seconds until softened. Lift it out and place on a tea towel. Unfold one of the pak choi leaves and put it in the centre of the pancake. Top with one-eighth of the vegetable mixture, keeping the matchstick strips facing as nearly as possible in the same direction. Add a couple of stems of coriander. Fold in the edges of the pancake, roll it up tightly and arrange in a dish. Repeat to make 8 pancakes in all. Cover with clingfilm and set aside. Serve within 1 hour.

4 Meanwhile, make the sauce. Put the chopped plums in a small saucepan with the water, cover and cook for 5 minutes until softened. Purée the plums with the soy sauce, then mix in the wasabi sauce and sugar to taste.

5 Arrange the pancakes on serving plates, garnish with the remaining coriander sprigs and serve with small bowls of the sauce to dip.

Fat 6 g
Carbohydrate 27 g
Protein 4 g
Energy 176 kcal (734 kj)

Rocket risotto

Preparation time **5 minutes**
Cooking time **20–25 minutes**
Serves **4**

1 teaspoon olive oil
1 onion, finely chopped
300 g (10 oz) arborio rice
1.2 litres (2 pints) vegetable stock
50 g (2 oz) rocket leaves
salt and pepper

1 Heat the oil in a large, nonstick frying pan or wok. Add the onion and fry for a few minutes until softened, then pour in the rice and stir well to coat the grains.

2 With the pan over a medium heat, gradually add the stock, a ladleful at a time. Stir while the stock is absorbed into the rice, and continue to add the stock a little at a time until it is all absorbed. This will take about 20 minutes.

3 Stir in the rocket, reserving 4 leaves for garnish, and cook briefly until the leaves start to wilt. Season to taste with salt and pepper. Serve each portion of risotto garnished with a rocket leaf.

Fat 1 g
Carbohydrate 63 g
Protein 6 g
Energy 290 kcal (1222 kj)

Orange and almond couscous salad

Preparation time **15 minutes**,
  plus standing
Cooking time **5 minutes**
Serves **6**

250 ml (8 fl oz) apple juice
175 g (6 oz) couscous
½ red pepper, cored, deseeded
  and diced
4 tablespoons chopped parsley
3 tablespoons chopped mint
25 g (1 oz) currants
2 oranges, segmented
1 red onion, sliced
25 g (1 oz) flaked almonds,
  to garnish

Citrus dressing
juice of 1 orange
juice of 1 lemon or lime
2 teaspoons olive or hazelnut oil
1 teaspoon clear honey

1 Place the apple juice in a saucepan and bring to the boil. Slowly stir in the couscous. Remove the pan from the heat, cover and leave to stand for 10 minutes. Fluff up the couscous with a fork.

2 Add the red pepper, herbs and currants to the couscous. Toss to combine. Transfer to a serving bowl and scatter over the orange segments and onion.

3 Make the dressing. Place all the ingredients in a small saucepan and heat gently to dissolve the honey. Do not allow the mixture to boil. Drizzle the dressing over the salad and serve it scattered with almonds.

Fat 4 g
Carbohydrate 32 g
Protein 4 g
Energy 170 kcal (720 kj)

Leek filo tarts

Preparation time **20 minutes**
Cooking time **30 minutes**
Serves **4**

8 sun-dried tomatoes
2 leeks, thinly sliced
300 ml (½ pint) white wine
2 tablespoons skimmed milk
1 small egg, separated
50 g (2 oz) low-fat soft cheese
12 pieces of filo pastry, each about
    15 cm (6 inches) square
salt and pepper

1 Put the tomatoes in a small bowl and pour over enough boiling water to cover. Set aside for 20 minutes.

2 Meanwhile, put the leeks in a saucepan with the white wine. Bring the wine to the boil and simmer until it has evaporated. Then remove the leeks from the heat and stir in the milk, egg yolk and cheese. Season to taste with salt and pepper.

3 Brush a pastry square with a little egg white and use it to line the base and sides of a 10 cm (4 inch) tart case. Brush two more squares and lay these on top, each at a slight angle to the first, allowing the edges to flop over the rim. Line 3 more tart cases in the same way to use up all the pastry squares.

4 Put a spoonful of the cooked leek mixture in each pastry case. Lay two rehydrated tomatoes on top of each tart and cover with the remaining leek mixture. Season again and cook in a preheated oven, 200°C (400°F), Gas Mark 6, for 20 minutes, covering the tarts with pieces of foil after 10 minutes.

Fat 5 g
Carbohydrate 7 g
Protein 5 g
Energy 135 kcal (565 kj)

Desserts

Cranberry ice

Preparation time **10 minutes**,
plus freezing
Cooking time **10 minutes**
Serves **4**

375 ml (13 fl oz) cranberry juice
100 g (3½ oz) caster sugar
125 g (4 oz) cranberries (thawed
if frozen)
3 tablespoons finely grated
orange rind

To decorate
mint sprigs
sugar-frosted cranberries

1 Put the cranberry juice and sugar in a saucepan and heat gently until the sugar has completely dissolved. Bring to the boil and simmer for 5 minutes. Remove the pan from the heat and stir in the cranberries and orange rind. Allow the mixture to cool completely.

2 Pour the mixture into a shallow container and place in the freezer until about 2.5 cm (1 inch) around the edge is firm. Turn the semi-frozen ice into a bowl, whisk well to break up the ice crystals, then return the mixture to the container and freeze until semi-frozen. Whisk once more and freeze again until firm. Alternatively, pour the chilled mixture into an ice-cream maker and churn until thick and frozen. Transfer to a container and freeze until firm.

3 Remove the cranberry ice from the freezer and allow to soften at room temperature for 15 minutes before serving. Scoop the ice into bowls and serve decorated with mint sprigs and sugar-frosted cranberries.

Fat 0 g
Carbohydrate 29 g
Protein 0 g
Energy 110 kcal (470 kj)

Mango sorbet with clementines

Preparation time **25 minutes**,
  plus freezing
Serves **6**

200 ml (7 fl oz) water
50 g (2 oz) light cane sugar
500 g (1 lb) clementines, about
  7 in all, halved
2 large mangoes
1 egg white
grated rind and juice of 1 lime

1 Put the measured water in a small saucepan and add the sugar. Bring gently to the boil and heat until the sugar has dissolved. Remove the pan from the heat and leave the syrup to cool.

2 Squeeze the juice from the clementines. Stone and peel one of the mangoes and purée the flesh until it is smooth. Stir the mango purée and clementine juice into the cooled sugar syrup and mix together.

3 Pour the mixture into a plastic container, cover and freeze for 2–3 hours until semi-frozen. Beat well with a fork or blitz in a food processor, then repeat the freezing and beating process. Mix in the egg white then freeze until solid. Alternatively, if you have an ice-cream maker, churn the mixture for 20–30 minutes until the sorbet is thick. Add the egg white and continue churning until the sorbet is well mixed and thick enough to scoop. Serve immediately or transfer to a plastic box and store in the freezer until required.

4 Take the sorbet out of the freezer and allow to soften at room temperature for 15 minutes before serving. Slice the remaining mango and toss the slices in the lime juice and rind mixture. Scoop the sorbet into dishes and serve with the mango slices.

Fat 0 g
Carbohydrate 23 g
Protein 2 g
Energy 95 kcal (404 kj)

Champagne granita with wild strawberries

Preparation time **25 minutes**,
  plus freezing
Serves **6**

40 g (1½ oz) light cane sugar
150 ml (¼ pint) boiling water
375 ml (13 fl oz) medium
  dry champagne
150 g (5 oz) alpine or
  wild strawberries

1 Stir the sugar into the boiling water until it has dissolved. Leave to cool.

2 Mix together the sugar syrup and champagne and pour the mixture into a shallow, nonstick baking tin so that it is no more than 2.5 cm (1 inch) deep.

3 Freeze the mixture for 2 hours until it is mushy, then break up the ice crystals with a fork. Return the mixture to the freezer for 2 more hours, beating every 30 minutes until it has formed fine, icy flakes.

4 To serve, spoon the granita and the strawberries into elegant glasses.

Fat 0 g
Carbohydrate 9 g
Protein 0 g
Energy 80 kcal (337 kj)

Pimm's jellies with iced lemonade

Preparation time **20 minutes**,
  plus chilling
Cooking time **4–5 minutes**
Serves **6**

3 tablespoons water
3 teaspoons powdered gelatine
1 dessert apple, cored and diced
1 tablespoon lemon juice
250 g (8 oz) strawberries, hulled
  and sliced
1 peach, halved, stoned and diced
1 orange, peeled and cut
  into segments
150 ml (¼ pint) Pimm's No. 1
450 ml (¾ pint) diet lemonade,
  chilled

To decorate
peach slices
strawberries, hulled and halved
mint sprigs or borage flowers
orange rind curls

1 Put the measured water in a small, heatproof bowl and sprinkle the gelatine over the top, making sure that all the powder is absorbed by the water. Leave to soak for 5 minutes. Stand the bowl in a small saucepan of gently simmering water so that the water comes halfway up the sides of the bowl. Heat for 4–5 minutes until the gelatine has dissolved and the liquid is clear.

2 Meanwhile, put the apple pieces in a bowl and toss with the lemon juice. Add the other fruits, mix together and divide among 6 glasses.

3 Stir the gelatine into the Pimm's and slowly mix in the lemonade. Pour the mixture over the fruit in the glasses. Transfer the jellies to the refrigerator and leave for at least 4 hours to chill and set.

4 Before serving, decorate the tops of the glasses with peach slices, strawberry halves, mint sprigs or borage flowers and orange rind curls. To make orange rind curls, use a canelle knife to pare away the rind in strips, then wrap the strips tightly around a skewer or the handle of a wooden spoon. Slide them off after a minute or two.

Fat 0 g
Carbohydrate 10 g
Protein 2 g
Energy 85 kcal (357 kj)

Minted zabaglione with blueberries

Preparation time **10 minutes**
Cooking time **7–8 minutes**
Serves **6**

4 egg yolks
3 tablespoons light cane sugar
125 ml (4 fl oz) sweet white wine
  or sherry
150 g (5 oz) blueberries, plus extra
  to decorate
4 teaspoons chopped mint, plus
  extra to decorate

1 Put the egg yolks and sugar in a large bowl set over a saucepan of simmering water. Use a hand-held electric whisk or a balloon whisk to beat the yolks and sugar for 2–3 minutes until they are thick and pale.

2 Whisk in the white wine or sherry, little by little, and continue whisking for about 5 minutes until the mixture is light, thick and foaming.

3 Warm the blueberries in a small saucepan with 1 tablespoon of water and spoon them into the bases of 6 small glasses. Whisk the mint into the foaming wine mixture and pour it over the blueberries. Stand the glasses on small plates or on a tray and arrange a few extra berries around them. Top with a little chopped mint and serve immediately.

Fat 3 g
Carbohydrate 10 g
Protein 2 g
Energy 85 kcal (356 kj)

Chinese spiced citrus salad

Preparation time **15 minutes**,
   plus chilling
Cooking time **15 minutes**
Serves **4**

3 oranges, peeled and pith
   removed, separated into
   segments
1 ruby grapefruit, peeled and
   pith removed, separated into
   segments
1 banana, thinly sliced
150 g (5 oz) low-fat crème fraîche,
   to serve

Syrup
1 whole clove
¼ teaspoon five spice powder
rind of 1 lime
1 vanilla pod, split lengthways
¼ teaspoon grated fresh
   root ginger
300 ml (½ pint) water

To decorate
1 tablespoon finely chopped mint
seeds of 1 pomegranate

1 Make the syrup. Combine all the ingredients in a
nonstick saucepan, bring to the boil and simmer gently
for 3–5 minutes. Remove the pan from the heat and
leave the syrup to infuse and cool.

2 Meanwhile, mix together the orange and grapefruit
segments in an attractive glass serving bowl. Add the
banana slices.

3 Pour the cooled syrup through a sieve to remove the
solids, then pour it over the fruits.

4 Leave the salad to chill in the refrigerator for 2–3
hours. Serve with crème fraîche and decorate with
finely chopped mint and pomegranate seeds.

Fat 6 g
Carbohydrate 25 g
Protein 4 g
Energy 163 kcal (688 kj)

Creole pineapple wedges

Preparation time **10 minutes**
Cooking time **8–10 minutes**
Serves **4**

1 small pineapple, about 1.25 kg
   (2½ lb)
1 tablespoon dark rum
juice of I lime
15 g (½ oz) sesame seeds

1 Cut the pineapple lengthways, first in half and then into quarters, leaving the leaves intact. The wedges should be about 1 cm (½ inch) thick, so it may be necessary to divide the quarters again.

2 Mix together the dark rum and lime juice and sprinkle the mixture over the pineapple slices.

3 Toast the pineapple under a preheated hot grill for 8–10 minutes, turning to ensure even cooking. Serve immediately, sprinkled with sesame seeds.

Fat 3 g
Carbohydrate 32 g
Protein 2 g
Energy 159 kcal (679 kj)

Baked saffron peaches with mango and cream

Preparation time **15 minutes**
Cooking time **15 minutes**
Serves **4**

2 large, slightly under-ripe
  peaches, halved and stoned
15 g (½ oz) pistachios, halved
a few saffron threads
a few drops of almond extract
30 g (1¼ oz) crunchy oat cereal
2 tablespoons orange juice
5 cm (2 inch) cinnamon stick,
  broken into 8 pieces

To serve
75 ml (3 fl oz) single cream
½ slightly under-ripe mango, thinly
  sliced
1 teaspoon grated dark chocolate
  (optional)

1 Scoop some of the flesh out of the peach halves and chop this finely. Put the halved peaches, skin side down, in a lightly oiled baking dish.

2 Mix together the chopped peach flesh, pistachios, saffron, almond extract, oat cereal and orange juice and spoon this mixture carefully into the peach halves.

3 Push the cinnamon pieces into the peach halves and bake the peaches, uncovered, in a preheated oven, 180°C (350°F), Gas Mark 4, for 15 minutes.

4 Carefully arrange one peach half on each dessert plate and pour some of the cream over one side of the peach. Serve with mango slices and a sprinkling of grated chocolate, if using.

Fat 6 g
Carbohydrate 16 g
Protein 3 g
Energy 130 kcal (547 kj)

Mango and pineapple pavlova

Preparation time **20 minutes**
Cooking time **1 hour**
Serves **4**

3 egg whites
175 g (6 oz) caster sugar
1 teaspoon strong black coffee
250 g (8 oz) very low-fat
    fromage frais
125 g (4 oz) mango, diced
125 g (4 oz) fresh pineapple, cut
    into chunks
1–2 passion fruits

1 Whisk the egg whites in a bowl until they are stiff.
Fold in 1 tablespoon sugar, then gradually whisk in the
remainder. The meringue must be glossy and form
peaks when spoonfuls are dropped into the bowl.
Fold in the black coffee.

2 Spread the meringue mixture over a large sheet
of baking parchment or greaseproof paper to form
a round about 20 cm (8 inch) across. Make a slight
hollow in the centre of the meringue and cook it in a
preheated oven, 120°C (250°F), Gas Mark ½, for
1 hour until crisp. Remove the meringue from the oven
and leave to cool on the paper for about 10 minutes
before peeling off the paper.

3 When the meringue is cold, fill the hollow in the top
with fromage frais. Arrange the mango and pineapple
on top, then scatter the passion fruit seeds and juice
over the fruit.

Fat 1 g
Carbohydrate 58 g
Protein 8 g
Energy 250 kcal (1069 kj)

Mini strawberry shortcakes

Preparation time **20 minutes**,
  plus chilling
Serves **4**

8 low-fat digestive biscuits
4 teaspoons low-sugar strawberry
  jam
250 g (8 oz) very low-fat cream
  cheese
2 teaspoons icing sugar
250 g (8 oz) strawberries
icing sugar, to decorate

1 Hull and slice the strawberries, reserving 4 for decoration. Fan the 4 reserved strawberries.

2 Spread a digestive biscuit with 1 teaspoon of the strawberry jam. Beat the cream cheese to soften and stir in the icing sugar, then spread one-quarter of the mixture over the biscuit. Lay a few strawberry slices on top of the cream cheese, then top with a second biscuit. Lay a fanned strawberry on top and dust with icing sugar.

3 Repeat to make 3 more shortcakes. Chill for a least 1 hour before serving.

Fat 5 g
Carbohydrate 29 g
Protein 7 g
Energy 187 kcal (789 kj)

Cheat's mango and passion fruit brûlée

Preparation time **10 minutes**,
plus chilling
Cooking time **2 minutes**
Serves **4**

1 small mango, peeled, stoned and
thinly sliced
2 passion fruit, flesh scooped out
300 g (10 oz) low-fat
natural yogurt
200 g (7 oz) crème fraîche
1 tablespoon icing sugar
a few drops vanilla essence
2 tablespoons demerara sugar

1 Divide the mango slices among 4 ramekins.

2 In a bowl, stir together the passion fruit flesh, yogurt, crème fraîche, icing sugar and vanilla essence, then spoon the mixture over the mango. Tap each ramekin to level the surface.

3 Sprinkle over the demerara sugar and cook the brûlées under a preheated hot grill for 1–2 minutes until the sugar has melted. Chill for about 30 minutes before serving.

Fat 5 g
Carbohydrate 19 g
Protein 5 g
Energy 131 kcal (541 kj)

Chocolate soufflé

Preparation time **8 minutes**
Cooking time **15 minutes**
Serves **6**

vegetable oil, for greasing
75 ml (3 fl oz) orange juice
75 g (3 oz) caster sugar
4 large egg whites
25 g (l oz) unsweetened
   cocoa powder
2 tablespoons orange liqueur
125 g (4 oz) low-fat vanilla ice
   cream, softened

1 Lightly grease 6 cups with the oil. In a small saucepan, heat the orange juice and sugar for 3–4 minutes over a medium-high heat, stirring occasionally until the mixture has a syrupy consistency. Remove the pan from the heat.

2 In a large bowl, beat the egg whites until they are stiff, but stop before dry peaks form. Pour the syrup over the egg whites and beat for 2 minutes. Add the cocoa and liqueur and beat briefly until well mixed.

3 Pour the mixture into the prepared cups and bake in a preheated oven, 220°C (425°F), Gas Mark 7, for 8-10 minutes or until the soufflés are puffed. Do not overcook or the soufflés will become tough.

4 Spoon 2 tablespoons of softened ice cream into the centre of each soufflé and serve immediately.

Fat 3 g
Carbohydrate 19 g
Protein 3 g
Energy 116 kcal (489 kj)

French apple flan

Preparation time **15 minutes**,
  plus chilling
Cooking time **35–40 minutes**
Serves **10**

150 g (5 oz) plain flour
50 g (2 oz) butter
50 g (2 oz) caster sugar
1 egg and 1 egg white,
  beaten together
a few drops vanilla extract
1 kg (2 lb) cooking apples,
  peeled, cored and thinly sliced
  and puréed
2 red-skinned dessert apples,
  thinly sliced
50 g (2 oz) caster sugar
4 tablespoons apricot jam
2 tablespoons lemon juice

1 Make the pastry. Sift the flour on to a cool work surface, make a well in the centre and add the butter, sugar, egg and egg white and vanilla extract. Using the fingertips of one hand, work these ingredients together, then draw in the flour. Knead lightly until smooth, then cover and chill for 1 hour.

2 Roll out the pastry thinly on a floured work surface and use it to line a lightly greased 25 cm (10 inch) fluted flan ring.

3 Fill the pastry case with the apple purée and arrange an overlapping layer of apple slices on top. Sprinkle with the sugar and bake in a preheated oven, 190°C (375°F), Gas Mark 5, for 35–40 minutes.

4 Meanwhile, heat the jam with the lemon juice. Strain the mixture and brush it over the apple slices. Serve the flan hot or cold.

Fat 5 g
Carbohydrate 41 g
Protein 3 g
Energy 211 kcal (889 kj)

Index

Acknowledgements

Executive Editor Sarah Ford
Project Editor Fiona Robertson
Art Director Geoff Fennell
Design Sue Michniewicz
Senior Production Controller
  Martin Croshaw
Picture Library Taura Riley

Octopus Publishing Group Limited/Frank Adam 19; /Stephen Conroy 2, 4, 5, 8-9, 29, 31, 39, 59, 67, 83, 109, 111, 113; /Sandra Lane 107; /Willaim Lingwood 96; /David Loftus 45; /Hilary Moore 123, 124; /Peter Myers 115; /Lis Parsons 1, 3, 7, 13, 21, 25, 27, 33, 34, 37, 47, 49, 63, 74, 77, 81, 85, 104-105, 117, 121; /William Reavell 53, 57, 101, 118; /Simon Smith 11, 15, 16, 40-41, 43, 51, 55, 61, 64-65, 69, 71, 72, 87, 88, 90-91, 93, 95, 99, 102; /Ian Wallace 79.